ALBERT KAHN ◆

ALBERT KAHN ◆

Builder of Detroit

Roger Matuz

Wayne State University Press
Detroit

Great Lakes Books
Detroit Biography Series for Young Readers

First Lady of Detroit: The Story of Marie-Thérèse Guyon, Mme. Cadillac,
by Karen Elizabeth Bush, 2001

The Reuther Brothers—Walter, Roy, and Victor,
by Mike Smith and Pam Smith, 2001

Willie Horton: Detroit's Own Willie the Wonder,
by Grant Eldridge and Karen Elizabeth Bush, 2001

Albert Kahn: Builder of Detroit, by Roger Matuz, 2002

Designed by Mary Primeau

Copyright© 2002 by Wayne State University Press, Detroit, Michigan 48201. All rights are reserved. No part of this book may be reproduced without formal permission. Manufactured in the United States of America.
06 05 04 03 02   5 4 3 2 1

Library of Congress Cataloging-in-Publication Data

Matuz, Roger.
   Albert Kahn : builder of Detroit / by Roger Matuz.
      p. cm. — (Detroit biography series for young readers)
   Summary: A biography of the German-born Jewish architect who, from the 1880s through the early 1940s, designed elegant homes, factories for Henry Ford, and industrial plants to support the United States' war effort.
   ISBN 0-8143-2956-X (cloth : alk. paper) — ISBN 0-8143-2957-8 (paper : alk. paper)
   1. Kahn, Albert, 1869-1942—Juvenile literature. 2. Architects—Michigan—Detroit—Biography—Juvenile literature. [1. Kahn, Albert, 1869-1942. 2. Architects.] I. Title. II. Series.
NA737.K28 M38 2002
720'.92—dc21   2001004169

Note: Wayne State University Press occupies the first floor of a building designed by Albert Kahn and built in 1913-14 for the B. F. Goodrich Tire Company on the northwest corner of Woodward and Hancock Avenues. The building has undergone many changes over the years, as Woodward Avenue was widened and the building changed hands. It was purchased by the university in 1989, renovated, and reopened in 1994.

For Mary Claire

CONTENTS

◆ 1 ◆

Hard Work (and a Little Luck)

"Albert," said Mr. Boyd.

Albert Kahn was often so focused on his work that he didn't notice what was going on around him. Boyd gave the fifteen-year-old boy a poke. Albert looked up.

"Mr. Mason wants to see you," continued Boyd. Albert put down his pencil and looked at his drawing, making a mental note of where he had stopped. He got up from his chair and followed Mr. Boyd, the office manager, into Mr. Mason's office. The year was 1884, and George Mason was part owner with Zacharias Rice of the Detroit architectural firm where Albert worked as a drafter. An architectural drafter draws a scale model of what a new building will look like.

After they entered the office, Mr. Boyd solemnly closed the door behind them.

"Albert, it has come to my attention that you might be color blind," said Mr. Mason. Albert said nothing as he tried to look surprised. He knew that being color blind was considered a handicap and could lead to his dismissal from the firm.

"As a test," suggested Mr. Mason, "why don't you identify the colors in the carpet, and point to them?"

Albert looked closely at the carpet that he had seen many times before. He was aware that there was a border that looked gray to him but was probably green or brown, colors he often had trouble telling apart. He began by pointing at and identifying an area of red, and then another of yellow. Then he came to the border. He paused for a second, took a breath, and said, "green."

"Thank you, Albert," said Mr. Mason. "You can go back to work now."

Albert turned, opened the door and closed it behind him. He walked back to his drafting table, a big desk where architects draw plans for buildings. As he picked up his pencil he breathed a sigh of relief. "Whew!" he said to himself. "I guess I guessed right." Then he went back to work. For one terrifying moment, his career as an architect was almost destroyed!

A week later, it was Mr. Mason's turn to try to get Albert's attention. Albert was hunched over and examining details of a house he had sketched. The owner wanted to add a room to the house and make another room larger.

"Albert. Albert. *Albert!*"

Albert Kahn looked up and realized he was being spoken to. "Yes, Mr. Mason?"

"Are you still working on that extra room?" asked Mr. Mason. "Leave it for now. It is six o'clock. Time to go home for dinner."

"But I think I'm on to something, sir," replied Albert, in his slight German accent. He would have that accent all of his life. "I will stop soon, and I will lock up the office when I leave. Enjoy your dinner, sir." Slowly his eyes drifted back to the drafting board.

Mr. Mason passed by the office later on his nightly walk after dinner. He noticed that a gaslight was still burning bright inside. Electric lights were only recently invented at that time and not widely used. Mr. Mason unlocked and opened the door of the building and went inside. He found Albert still working at his desk.

Mr. Mason walked quietly over to Albert's work space. Albert was concentrating so hard on his work that he did not notice Mr. Mason. Finally, Albert looked up. "I almost have it figured out, Mr. Mason." His drawing showed how a single outside wall could be moved to create enough space to make one larger room and a new room as well.

A typical day in the life of Albert Kahn—shirtsleeves rolled up, a pencil in his hand, plans spread out on his desk, at work. *Albert Kahn Associates, Inc., Architects & Engineers*

Mr. Mason looked over the details and nodded. "I see. And even though the building is larger, it still has a graceful appearance."

"I want to make the rooms more useful," Albert agreed. "That is the problem I am working on."

As Albert walked home that night he felt happy with his work. He paused in front of a butcher's shop near his family home. It was dark, but he noticed a sign hanging in the window. It said BOY WANTED.

A year ago, that same sign hung in that same window. Albert almost had taken the job. That was after he had been dismissed from an architectural firm where he worked as an errand boy. The owner told Albert that he was good for running errands and emptying wastebaskets but definitely did not have the talent to be an architect.

Albert remembered how bad he had felt back then. It seemed that his dreams of becoming an architect were never going to come true. Maybe he wasn't as good at drawing as he thought.

Instead, his luck turned. Shortly after being fired he was invited to take drawing classes given by an artist named Julius Melchers. Mr. Melchers noticed Albert's drawing abilities and recommended him to Mr. Mason. Before long, Albert was running errands for some new bosses—Mr. Mason and Mr. Rice. Soon, they gave him chances to trace, and then to draw architectural plans, and they were pleased with his work.

In his spare time at the office, Albert studied books on architecture in the firm's library. He would continue to study throughout his life. "There is always so much to learn," he told Mr. Mason back then. "The world is advancing so very fast."

Albert began to receive regular drawing assignments from Mason & Rice and was paid $3.50 per week, or about $15 a month. After a year, his salary was doubled to $30 per month. In those days, $30 was worth much more than it is today. Albert used his new income to help feed his family, which

A portion of Woodward Avenue seen from the foot of Michigan Avenue in the late 1880s. Electric lighting had only recently been invented. One of the city's first light towers is seen in the foreground, at the street corner. Streetcars were still pulled by horses.

The front right part of the picture shows the lawn of the old City Hall, where a display is set up. The large building in the center of the picture would be replaced in 1922 by the National Bank of Detroit building, designed by Albert Kahn. The Soldiers and Sailors Monument, in front of the building in the upper left corner, still stands. *Courtesy of the Burton Historical Collection, Detroit Public Library*

included five younger brothers and two younger sisters. Now he could afford to buy meat at this same butcher's shop where he almost took a job.

Albert turned away from the butcher shop and continued home. When he entered the house he saw his father, Joseph, sitting at the dinner table counting the money he made that day. Joseph sold vegetables from a cart pulled by an old horse. Every morning, Joseph had to walk a few miles up Woodward Avenue to where the horse was stabled and the cart was loaded. Joseph made some extra money by also selling vegetables he grew in his own backyard garden. He had bought seeds for the garden from the nearby Ferry Seed Company of Detroit. At that time—the 1880s—it was the largest seed company in the world. The Ferry Seed Company was the first to market packets of seeds especially for city gardeners. The seeds were taken from plants grown in fields where the Detroit Medical Center is now located.

"Good evening, Albert," said his father. "Or should I say, good morning—since it is almost midnight? There is a plate of food for you warming in the oven."

Albert was tired, but he sat with his father and ate dinner. His father asked him about work. Both Albert and his father had been busy. They hadn't had a chance to talk lately. Albert told Joseph about the two new rooms he had designed. He also told his father about the incident a week before, when he was being tested to see if he was color blind.

"If I had guessed brown," he told his father, "I would be working for the butcher today!" Albert finished eating, went to the kitchen to wash his plate, said good night to his father, and then headed for bed.

◆ 2 ◆

From Child Prodigy to Child Laborer

Things had not always gone that well for Albert Kahn and his family. They had faced many hard times.

Albert was born in Rhaunen, Germany, in 1869. Albert, the oldest child, had three brothers and two sisters by the time he was ten years old. There would eventually be eight Kahn children. They often had to move from place to place. Joseph didn't always have steady work. He was a Rabbi, and he traveled around to many small towns to serve people and teach the principles of the Jewish religion. His stays were sometimes only for a few days. If he stayed longer, the family would move into a house in the new town for a few weeks.

Joseph was a dreamer. He liked making big plans, but somehow the plans never seemed to work out the way he imagined they would.

The life of constantly moving from one village of western Germany to another was the only life Albert knew until he was five years old, when Joseph and Rosalie, Albert's mother, decided the family should settle in one place. Joseph would continue to travel for work and serve as a Rabbi.

The family—along with Rosalie's sister Ethel—moved to a house in Luxembourg, in a village called Echternach in a very scenic valley with forests and streams and mountains nearby, not far from where Albert was born. Luxembourg is surrounded by Germany on the south and east and by Belgium on the north and west, with a southern part also bordering France.

Like Albert's mother, Aunt Ethel was a small woman who liked music and art. Aunt Ethel had a piano, and she encouraged Albert to learn to play. He was shy at first, but he began to teach himself until he was able to play a few notes and form a song.

Aunt Ethel insisted that he take piano lessons. Albert quickly became such a good pianist that he was considered a prodigy—a natural talent—by some of the villagers.

For five years the Kahn family stayed in Luxembourg. Still, the family never had much money for food and clothing. Joseph Kahn decided that he had to find steady work.

Family friends had emigrated to the United States and found better opportunities than they had in Germany or Luxembourg. Joseph and Rosalie talked about how much better off the family would be in America. They decided that Joseph would go ahead, and the family would join him after he was settled. Meanwhile, everyone in the family began to learn how to speak English.

On the morning Joseph prepared to leave, he took Albert for a walk in the valley. The morning air was fresh. Joseph told Albert about the journey he was taking—how important it was and how much he would miss his family. He couldn't wait for them to join him in Baltimore, Maryland, where he was headed. He and Albert stopped to sit on a bench at the side of the road.

"Albert," Joseph said to his son. "Whatever happens, don't be afraid."

"I'm not afraid, papa."

"Albert," his father said, "when I am gone, you are the head of the family. You need to help your mama and your aunt around the house, and help take care of your brothers and sisters. You are nine years old, soon to be ten. You still have much to learn, but you can also show what you have learned. Be good and help out around home whenever you can—*before* you are asked. Soon we will all be together again in a new and magical place. Life won't be so hard."

Albert worked hard around the house and had time to continue his piano lessons. He began playing recitals in front of small audiences. He also began to enjoy drawing, but his teachers didn't show as much enthusiasm for his art work as they did for his musical talent. He worked very hard at being more precise in his drawings of trees, houses, and things inside houses—like the piano, or a vase with flowers. And he found that when he concentrated on details he enjoyed drawing even more: it was like putting musical notes together to form a song. Though his teachers noticed improvement in his drawing, they still thought his best talent was as a musician.

During the summer of Albert's eleventh year, the Kahn family received news from Joseph that they should plan to join him. Albert helped his mother prepare for the journey. They packed as many clothes and kitchen items as they could into a large trunk. Albert led the family on to a train. His mother followed from behind, making sure that all of the children were in front of her, and in her sight. The family rode by train to Paris, France, and then northwest to Le Havre, a small, seaside town, where they boarded a boat to England. They arrived in Southampton, where they got on a large ship, bound for America.

During the voyage Albert barely had time to feel excited or sad. He helped care for his brothers and sisters, playing with them and keeping them safe on board the ship. When he had free time, Albert liked to go to the front of the boat and look out.

He already began seeing and learning new things: he watched the sailors working, and he learned how to eat corn on the cob. Where Albert came from, corn was used to feed animals—the kernels were small and hard. The corn they ate on the boat was sweet and moist. Everything seemed new on this exciting journey!

The boat landed in New York. Papa was there and helped them as they met with American officials. Albert had learned a little English back home, but people here spoke too fast. He was glad his father could manage things, and he was proud when his father hugged him and said, "My little man, you have done very well."

The family stayed in Baltimore for a few weeks. Then Joseph informed them that they were going to move to Detroit, where some family friends had settled, and Joseph and Rosalie would work in a restaurant.

After a long train ride and then a boat ride on a lake that seemed as big as the ocean, the family stepped down to a busy dock on the Detroit River. A family friend was there to greet them. The family loaded up their belongings and hopped on the man's wagon, which was pulled by a horse. They rode from the dock to a small house. In no time the family unpacked, ate dinner, and were all soon asleep in their new home.

Early the next morning, Albert was awakened by his father. "Come with me," he whispered, and he put a finger to his mouth to show that Albert should be quiet. Albert dressed, drank some milk, and went with his father to a large building. There, in a small restaurant, Albert was given a broom and he began to sweep the floor.

People came to the restaurant to eat before they went off to work. Some spoke German, others English, and some spoke Polish or Italian. At first Albert was shy, but he learned to speak English from his patient father and from customers. He was kept busy cleaning tables and washing dishes.

Albert worked with his father in the restaurant for over a year. Although he was only twelve, he hadn't gone to school in America, and he never would. He didn't have time to play piano anymore, either. There was work to be done. The family barely had enough money for food and clothing.

The restaurant was located in a large and busy train station in Detroit. Whenever he could, Albert watched the big locomotives chugging in, pulling train cars filled with people. The people came from all over, but the railroad cars, he learned, were built in Detroit. During the 1880s, trains brought many vacationers to Michigan. Summer boat cruises on the Great Lakes were very popular.

Then one day his father announced that the restaurant

was going to be closed. Though the train station was busy, not enough people stopped in the restaurant to eat. Joseph took an opportunity to serve as a Rabbi far off in Florida. He returned after three months, and then he was off to Trenton, New Jersey, for six more months. When he returned from New Jersey, Joseph worked as a salesman. First he sold spectacles, then sewing machines, and then vegetables.

After the restaurant closed, Albert worked as a stable boy, cleaning up after horses, brushing them, and walking them around. He continued drawing and became as good at drawing as he had been as a pianist. His father and mother encouraged Albert to draw. Even though the family didn't have much money, Albert was given a drawing board and pencils and paper for his thirteenth birthday.

Rosalie, Albert's mother, enjoyed art and had a circle of friends who met regularly to talk about art. One of her friends introduced Rosalie to an architect named John Scott. Rosalie showed him some of Albert's drawings, and Mr. Scott invited Albert to work for his architectural firm.

Albert was overjoyed: he was thirteen years old and had a job where he could get paid for doing what he liked best—drawing. Or so he thought. For at work, Albert's job was to empty wastebaskets and to grind ink. The ink was for the drawings used to make copies of blueprints. Albert took blocks of ink hardened by chemicals and placed them in a machine where they passed through rollers and turned into powder for copies or liquid for drawing. It was a messy job.

Albert was not encouraged to talk to architects and only occasionally had time to look at books on architecture in the library. When he was finally given a chance to draw, Mr. Scott did not like his sketches. Soon, Albert began working at the firm only in the afternoons; mornings he worked at the stable. Finally, Mr. Scott told Albert that he was going to hire someone to replace him, someone who he thought had a more promising future in architecture than Albert.

Instead of going home that afternoon, Albert walked around the neighborhood. He felt sick, and he didn't want to tell his family that he had been fired. As six o'clock approached, he sat on a street corner near his house. He wondered what he would tell his family.

"Hello, Albert," came the cheery voice of a passerby.

Albert looked up. "Oh, hello, Mr. Melchers." It was Julius Melchers, an artist and a family friend. Albert's mother liked him because he was an excellent sculptor who liked to talk about art. Mr. Melchers had also come to Detroit from Germany.

"You look sad, Albert."

Albert told Mr. Melchers about his problem. Mr. Melchers assured him that it was not the end of the world. That made Albert feel a little better, but when he came home and saw the large family cramped in the small house he felt as if he had really let his family down. Albert went to sleep early, but he awoke during the night to think about what he should do.

He worked all the next day at the stable. That night, when Albert told his parents about his change of luck, his mother suggested that he take drawing classes with Mr. Melchers. A few family friends took classes with him on Sunday evenings, she noted. On Sundays Albert didn't have to work at the stables. He decided to go to the drawing class. He admired Mr. Melchers.

Julius Melchers arrived in America twenty years before Albert was born. He came from an area of Germany ruled by members of the royal Hohenzoller family for almost 700 years. In the late 1840s, rebellions against royalty spread throughout Europe—to France, Hungary, and Germany. Mr. Melchers joined those who called for greater freedom and more of a say in government. Many rebels were jailed for protesting, and some were killed. Melchers was in danger and decided to travel to America, where he could live freely and work as an artist.

Albert didn't understand much of what Mr. Melchers said in his art classes. He talked a lot about ideas and feelings. Albert concentrated on drawing with strong lines and fine details with precision. His work seemed different from the others, but Mr. Melchers praised his drawings. After a few weeks, Mr. Melchers stopped Albert after class and they talked.

"Albert," he said, "I have noticed your work is much more

precise and exact than that of my other students. May I ask why you like to draw?"

"I do it for enjoyment," said Albert, "but I want it to be useful." He explained that he liked to draw the way he enjoyed playing piano—to play a song precisely, to honor its melody. Mr. Melchers said he understood. "You are color blind, too, eh?" Mr. Melchers stated. "Not a good thing for a painter, but you are a true drawer."

Albert was concerned that Mr. Melchers might suggest that this class was not right for him. Instead, Mr. Melchers said, "I have recommended you to George Mason. He is an architect and has a company with a partner. You would start there as an errand boy, but they have a nice library where you can study and draw in your spare time. If you keep busy, learn, and continue to draw with precision, you will be given a chance to develop."

Albert thought about it for a moment; he felt a sense of fear that he might relive the disappointment he had with Mr. Scott. "Do you think I'm good enough?" he asked Mr. Melchers.

"It matters first that *you* think you're good enough," came the reply. "If you have doubts, maybe you aren't, but how will you know unless you try? If I had doubts I wouldn't have recommended you to Mr. Mason. Albert, you have talent, but you have to have *chutzpah,* too—you have to dare to take risks. Listen: It takes a live fish to swim upstream. Any dead fish can go with the current."

Albert had just recently stopped working again as a stable-boy and was intending to try to get a job with a butcher the next morning. Instead, he had another chance to try and make it as an architect. He thanked Mr. Melchers and assured him that he would work hard.

Albert did work hard, first at the routine tasks of emptying wastebaskets, cleaning and sweeping, and grinding ink. Soon, he was encouraged to use the firm's library. Architects looked at his drawings and made helpful suggestions. He was taught how to present buildings in drawings from several different perspectives, also known as *points of view.* Soon he was given

The Gilbert Lee House, built in 1888, at Ferry Street and John R. This was the first house designed entirely by Albert Kahn. *Courtesy of the Burton Historical Collection, Detroit Public Library*

assignments. And within a year, at age fifteen, he was a full-time architect.

Those were happy times. Albert was given increasing responsibilities. He made friends with other architects and with Mr. Mason, who often invited him to dinner. Mr. Mason had a large house on the corner of Dequindre and Congress. Dinners with the Mason family were formal, with servants, linen table cloths and napkins, and fine plates and silverware. It was so different from the dinners Albert was used to at home. After dinner, Mr. Mason would show him photographs and illustrations, pointing out details that Albert should con-

The office and staff of Mason & Rice in July of 1888. Albert is nearest the camera. George Nettleton *(second closest man in the foreground)* would go into business with Albert in 1896. George Mason is seated in back on the far right. Drafting tables, where architects work, are shown in the picture. *Courtesy of the Burton Historical Collection, Detroit Public Library.*

sider in his designs. He talked about what kinds of architectural features worked well on certain kinds of buildings, and what was less successful, or simply showy, and not useful.

Albert's work progressed so quickly that he was soon given the assignment of designing a new house. He met with Mr. Gilbert Lee, who hired the firm of Mason & Rice to design his new home. As Mr. Lee explained what he wanted in the house—how many bedrooms, for example—Albert *sketched*, rather than taking notes. That was his special method: sketching the details. From those sketches he would make many improvements until the drawing and plans were perfect.

Albert Kahn loved to draw. On the drawing board he could design buildings that were attractive and useful. He could solve problems—making sure that walls and floors were strong enough and that many windows could be included. On the drawing board things could be made to make sense, and work, and be beautiful.

Albert completed details on the Gilbert Lee House. He was given regular assignments at Mason and Rice over the next five years. When he was twenty, he entered an architecture magazine contest for a scholarship to study in Europe. Many months after he had entered the contest, he came home from work one day and his mother casually mentioned that the postman had delivered a letter for him. She left the letter on his bed.

"I'll look at it after I eat," replied Albert.

"Very well," she said, adding, "but it's from *American Architect* magazine. Aren't they the ones who—" Before she could finish, Albert raced off to his room, which he shared with his brothers Gustav and Julius. They were busy studying. He found the letter on his bed and opened it. He shouted "Hooray!" He had won a $500 scholarship to study in Europe. Julius and Gustav jumped for joy, too, then the other kids joined in, and so did their parents.

◆ 3 ◆

A Real Education

Soon, Albert was back on a ship, crossing the Atlantic Ocean. Only this time, the ship was traveling east, from America to Europe. The earlier journey across the Atlantic was one of uncertainty: a new world, a new language, a different culture. But after much hard work and tough times when his family had little money, Albert could now feel better about the journey ahead.

The ship landed in Southampton, England. Albert strapped on a backpack filled with clothes and drawing materials and began walking to the train station. The pack was heavy on his back, but he managed.

Albert was a small man, barely five feet tall, but his shoulders were strong. He was glad he decided to take the backpack rather than a suitcase; the suitcase could hold more items, but it was more difficult to walk with than a pack. By walking to the train station instead of paying for a horse carriage ride, Albert was able to save a few pennies.

The train took him to London, where Albert was to attend three weeks of architecture classes. Before the classes began, Albert enjoyed two weeks of sketching buildings in London, including Big Ben (a large clock tower), Parliament (the British government building), and Westminster Abbey (England's greatest church in the Gothic style of architecture).

American Architect magazine had arranged for the classes. As part of his scholarship from the magazine, Albert was required to mail sketches each month from the various towns he traveled to in Europe.

Albert eagerly completed his sketches, but in the class-room he had to force himself to pay attention. Without think-ing, he would take out his jackknife and begin whittling a pencil point, or start drawing a building he saw out of one of the classroom windows.

After two weeks of classes, Albert politely informed the teacher that he was no longer going to attend. "I learn by doing," he explained. The teacher invited Albert to tea to dis-cuss his plans. He recommended several buildings for Albert to sketch, then added, "It's a miserable autumn here in London. Soon it will be winter. If you want to learn about architecture by sketching buildings, you might as well go where it is warmer."

"Where would you suggest?" Albert asked.

"Well, perhaps you should begin in Italy, or Greece."

Albert considered the suggestion. It made sense in many ways to stay in warmer weather: he wouldn't have to buy heav-ier clothes or gloves, and he could move around more easily. The next day he made arrangements to travel by train to Dover, where he could get on a boat to cross the sea channel between England and France. Then he went by train through France and on to Rome in Italy.

Being in Rome was wonderful, but overwhelming, with its crowds of people, and so much to see, so much history. Albert sketched a few sites, including the Arch of Constantine, and then decided to move on. He needed quieter places where he could study the details of buildings and capture them in his sketches.

He went hiking north, along roads and over bridges that were built almost two thousand years earlier. He arrived in Siena, a much smaller city than Rome but with plenty of examples of excellent architecture of the Italian Renaissance. The Renaissance is a period of history that began a few decades before Columbus arrived in the New World in 1493. It was a time when art and architecture flourished, as artists and architects used classic styles of the past to create new and beautiful works.

Laid out over three hills, Siena was designed as a walled city to keep out intruders in times of war. It has not changed much since those days. Siena has seventeen neighborhoods, each with its own church. And it has a grand public square with a magnificent building—il Pubblico (which means "public building")—built before the Renaissance. Albert sketched in Siena for two weeks.

However, Albert was still feeling bewildered, as he had in Rome. He could make his way well enough by using maps. He could communicate well enough: he learned a bit of Italian, and he found people who spoke English or German. But the buildings and their many fine details were overwhelming—so beautiful, and so elaborate.

From Siena he traveled north to Florence, which had been the center of the Italian Renaissance. Some of the buildings of Florence are like fortresses, from which the city was defended, and are examples of the earliest style of the Italian Renaissance. Albert was sketching the Uffizi Palace, a U-shaped structure built during the 1500s that was originally an office building ("uffizi" means "office" in Italian) and later, in 1591, became a museum. As he was sketching, he met a fellow traveling student.

The student invited Albert to dinner, and soon they were joined by several of the student's friends. It was a time for merriment, for one of the students was returning home to France the next day. Albert allowed himself a modest meal and a drink, then politely got up to go. Just then, another friend of the student's arrived. He was also carrying a large sketchbook. The new arrival immediately ordered more food for everyone at the table. Albert was introduced as "a good sketcher" to the new arrival.

The young man stood up and shook Albert's hand. "Hello, I'm Henry Bacon."

"Hello, I'm Albert Kahn."

"What did you sketch today?" asked Bacon.

"The Uffizi Palace," replied Albert.

"Oh, yes, a bit tricky, eh?—with the top floor that juts out." Bacon reached over to the table and opened his sketchbook. He flipped a few pages until he found the one he wanted. "Yes, I think I managed to catch the top floor gallery." Albert examined the sketch closely and was astounded at how well it was done. "It is an excellent sketch," he said to Bacon.

27

"Oh, thank you. Once I was able to see how the walls support the upper floor, I understood the overall design. Well, won't you stay?"

"No. I thank you, but I must be off," replied Albert.

"Have you sketched at the Fortezza Belvedere yet?" asked Bacon.

"No," replied Albert, "but I plan to, soon."

"I'm told you can see the best views of Florence from there," continued Bacon. "Well, then, let's meet there tomorrow afternoon, say 2:00? We can have a go at it and compare sketches."

"Good," replied Albert. "I will see you there tomorrow."

The sketch Albert saw of Bacon's was very good. Albert stopped to look at his own sketch. It was fine, too, but he was interested in the different details Bacon used to show the top floor.

The next morning Albert sketched at the Uffizi again. Then he crossed a bridge over the Arno River and had fruit for lunch as he walked through the beautiful Baboli Gardens near the Fortezza. He arrived at the Fortezza by noon, wanting to look it over fully before Bacon arrived. The Fortezza was impressive. Originally built as a fortress to help protect the town of Florence, it was now used as an art museum. It gave Albert some interesting ideas about how a building could be massive yet still have a graceful appearance. Albert began sketching.

Bacon soon arrived. He and Albert greeted each other, and then each began sketching from different angles. They compared sketches and discussed their drawings over dinner. They were quickly becoming friends.

Bacon had won a major scholarship to study and travel in Europe. He had been there for nearly two years. Bacon described to Albert the places he had visited. He had traveled as far as Greece and had stayed in fine hotels and villas throughout his trip. Bacon invited Albert to travel with him to Northern Italy and France as he made his way back to London, where Bacon was due in June for two weeks before returning home to America.

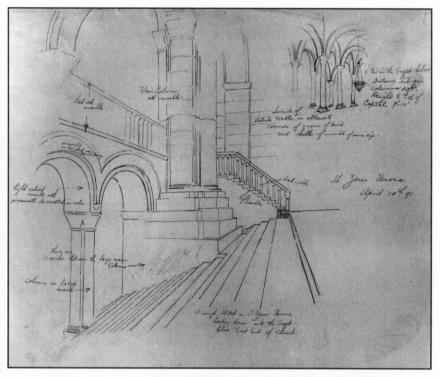

A sketch Albert made inside a church, St. Zeno, in Verona, Italy, during his walking tour of Europe. The sketch is dated April 24, 1891. Courtesy of the University of Michigan Museum of Art. *Transferred from the College of Architecture and Design. Gift of the Family of Albert Kahn: through Dr. Edgar A. Kahn; Mrs. Barnett Malbin; Mrs. Martin L. Butzel, 1972/2.698*

Albert declined Bacon's offer to travel with him: "I couldn't afford to stay at the places you stay and eat and drink as you do."

"I'm not sure how long I can afford it either," admitted Bacon. "But I think we're both learning so much and I feel that I'm beginning to make the most of this scholarship."

A couple of days later they finished another sketch in Florence. Albert prepared to say goodbye. Bacon again asked Albert to join him.

"That would be great," replied Albert. "But I can't afford to travel any other way than the way I do."

"Tell you what," said Bacon. "You can be in charge of the finances. We'll do it your way as a general plan. I have connections in several places; if they put us up for free, or for a cheap rate, we'll stay; if not, well, then, you can decide."

And so they hiked and sketched and talked and hiked and sketched and talked, from February to June, from Florence to Paris. Later in life, whenever Albert talked about his experience with Bacon, he would say, "we strapped on our backpacks and walked right out of Florence to the next town. Together we traveled, and he taught me."

From Florence they hiked north through mountains and reached the town of Bologna. They hiked northeast to the town of Padua, and then reached Venice in late March. They stayed for two weeks in Venice, a city built on the banks of a lagoon. Venice has many examples of Renaissance architecture, and other styles as well. Bacon could show Albert two-story palaces dating back to the eleventh century, or Renaissance architecture from the sixteenth century. Venice had been a powerful republic, but it fell from power in the sixteenth century and became frozen in time, like a vast museum.

Albert and Henry left Venice in early April to travel across northern Italy to reach France. They stopped in the town of Verona, where they sketched beautiful structures that were built before the Renaissance. Bacon was amazed at Kahn's precision at drawing and his organization as a traveler. Kahn marveled at Bacon's resourcefulness at drawing and his knowledge of history and architectural styles. Bacon seemed to know the history and architecture of every place they visited. He could point out the slightest differences from one building to another. And he liked to talk, and went on talking through the entire journey.

Along the way, Albert enjoyed what he called his "real education." Through Bacon's talks he could make sense of the different styles of architecture from different time periods. Albert would later use some of the details he sketched in designs back in Detroit. For example, his design for the conservatory on

The Conservatory on Belle Isle is a domed structure made of glass and ornamental steel. Sunlight reflecting off of glass is common in Kahn-designed buildings. Albert was inspired to design a domed structure after having seen and sketched several in Italy. *Courtesy of Meadows & Co. Photography*

Belle Isle, where plants from all over the world are on display, has an arched dome of glass supported by ornamental iron. The conservatory hints of the famous stone domes that were built in Italy during the Renaissance.

Albert and Henry passed from Italy into France. They stayed several days in the city of Bourges, in the center of France, with the family of a French student Bacon had met in Florence. The family invited Albert to return later during his trip. Albert and Henry followed a river into the Loire Valley, where there are many old castles—including a real castle that inspired the fairy tale *Sleeping Beauty*. Albert and Henry criss-crossed the valley, following the Loire River, to sketch details of many large houses on grand estates built during the French Renaissance. Such a home is called a chateau in French (or chateaux, when referring to more than one). Finally, the two young men made their way to Paris.

In Paris they observed and sketched the old buildings— the cathedral of Notre Dame, the palace of Versailles—as well as new buildings, including the Eiffel Tower, which was only a year old at the time of their visit. They attended an exhibition by famous artists associated with the Ecole des Beaux Arts (The School of Fine Arts). Henry Bacon was captivated by their work, but Albert, though impressed, was not as approving.

"The drawings are amazingly good, don't you think?" said Bacon.

"They show great technical skill," agreed Albert.

"It's inspiring to me. It makes me want to be more creative."

"But," asked Albert, "what purpose do they have? I mean the drawings and designs are spectacular and imaginative, but what for? They can't be transferred from paper to reality. They aren't useful in any way."

"Well," laughed Bacon, "some things are just beautiful. They might not make sense or have immediate purpose, but they can still be pleasing to the eye, and the imagination."

"Yes, I suppose," said Albert. "But I like things to be part of reality, and useful. I'm not saying the designs aren't impressive . . ."

Bacon laughed again and slapped Albert on the back. "You're so serious, my friend . . . such a serious person."

Albert didn't argue. To Albert, being useful was beautiful.

A sketch by Albert of a chateau in Chenonceaux, France, made on September 28, 1891. The different shapes of roofs, the bays, and the decorative features inside (including elegant fireplaces, stairways, and furniture) were elements Albert would begin using in designs when he returned to Detroit. *Courtesy of the University of Michigan Museum of Art. Transferred from the College of Architecture and Design, Gift of the Family of Albert Kahn: through Dr. Edgar A. Kahn; Mrs. Barnett Malbin; Mrs. Martin L. Butzel, 1972/2.556*

Paris was the last stop on their tour together. Bacon boarded a train out of town, and Albert still had several months ahead in Europe. Albert and Henry Bacon remained friends for the rest of their lives, though their paths would cross only occasionally. A little more than twenty years after their tour, Henry Bacon began working on his most famous project—the Lincoln Memorial in Washington, D.C.—which would be completed in 1922.

Meanwhile, Albert's journey continued. He traveled northeast, and back in time. Albert returned to the area of Luxembourg that he had left ten years earlier. He visited relatives there, including Aunt Ethel, and he sketched farmhouses and castles, taking in the beauty of the hills and valleys, rivers and forests. He was seeing his old home in a new way—through the eyes of an architect.

Then he went into Germany, where he traveled during July and early August. Features of German architecture he sketched, especially heavy columns and arches, were used in his design of the Detroit News building completed in 1916. The columns and arches provide a dignified appearance, appropriate for a newspaper office, while the massive building housed a huge production operation printing the daily paper. In Munich, Germany, he sketched a factory where iron was produced. He sketched castles and houses as well as factory buildings during his time in Germany.

Moving east from Germany Albert passed through Belgium and sketched the architecture of the Flemish style, a term that describes art of the Middle Ages when the area we now know as Belgium and the Netherlands was called Flanders. Then Albert returned to France. He passed through Paris and returned to the Loire valley, where he made many sketches of the French chateauesque style, rectangular buildings with jutting bays. A bay is a rounded extension of a wall, providing additional space to a room inside; usually these small areas have windows, called *bay windows*.

Albert liked the different kinds of roofs of the French Renaissance style: the chateaux had steep, large, rectangular roofs that were contrasted with the rounded roofs of the bays. Many of these elements would later appear in several of his designs back home. He was learning by doing—that's why he called it "a real education."

Albert completed his journey by swinging north. First he traveled in Brittany, the northwest region of France, and then through Normandy, the northern coast region of France where his final French destination, the port city of Le Havre, is located. There, he boarded a boat across to Southampton, England, and then boarded another ship for a long crossing of the Atlantic Ocean and his return home—to Detroit.

◆ 4 ◆

Small Things Lead to
Bigger Things

Albert returned from Europe to good things in Detroit. His family was healthy and busy: Julius and Moritz were in a Detroit public high school, and Papa was helping to run a saloon.

After a happy reunion at home, Albert enjoyed a happy return to work. Mr. Mason was impressed by the sketches Albert had sent from Europe. About ten years earlier, Mason had toured and sketched his way through Europe. Albert talked about his journey with everyone who wanted to hear, and he began living on his own. He rented an apartment on John R Street.

Soon, Mr. Mason promoted Albert to Office Manager. Albert was responsible for assigning work and overseeing the bookkeeping, or accounting. Managing money, being well-organized, and drawing with precision—the things he had learned as a boy and practiced on his European trip—came into use every day.

Julius graduated from high school the following year and enrolled at the University of Michigan. Albert helped pay for his classes and helped Julius move to Ann Arbor. While Julius registered for classes one day, Albert walked around the campus looking at buildings and—as always—sketching. Afterward, the Kahn brothers stopped for a Vernor's ice cream float. Then they walked to the train depot, where Albert would board a train to take him back to Detroit. He arrived in the same station where he once worked in a restaurant. He had come a long way since then, and there were new worlds ahead, new worlds to draw, and new worlds to build.

Albert began to use some of the architectural styles he had observed and sketched in Europe. These stylistic touches became part of the functional design he matched to the tastes of a client and the purpose of a building. For example, the large house that William Livingston wanted to build on Elliot Street in Detroit reminded Albert of a chateau he had studied in the Loire Valley of France. Albert incorporated elements of the French *chateauesque* style—double windows that were large and square, an archway over the front door, and a bay jutting out from the building and capped with a rounded, cone-shaped roof that complemented the larger, steep, rectangular roof.

For Mr. Watson Freer's house, on the other hand, Albert included details from Italian Renaissance architecture. Freer was an art collector and wanted large, museum-like rooms with lots of marble—similar to Italian architecture. The Freer house, which has large single windows with rounded arches above them and a balcony with ornate metal work that Albert created, was built on Ferry Street, near the Detroit Institute of Arts. The house is now part of the Merrill-Palmer Institute.

Albert also designed interiors of homes and offices. The offices of Hiram Walker and Sons, built in Windsor, Ontario, in 1894 by Mason and Rice, includes fireplaces based on sketches Albert made in villas in Venice, Italy, and chateaux in Orleans, France. The exterior, meanwhile, incorporates elements of a palace he sketched in Florence, Italy. Ten years later, Albert designed a mansion for one of the Walker sons, E. Chandler Walker. That mansion was later used for many years as the Art Gallery of Windsor.

Two other projects Albert completed during this period— from 1893 to 1896—proved to have lasting influences on his life. One was a simple redesign and restoration of an older house. He was hired for the job by an acquaintance of Henry Joy, a young businessman. Even though the work wasn't difficult for Albert, he treated it with the same dedication he did for any other project—big or small.

The William Livingston house (1893) features a bay with a cone-shaped roof. The design was inspired by the chateaux Albert had sketched while touring in France (look at Albert's drawing on p. 33). Compare this house, designed after Albert returned from Europe, with the Lee house pictured on page 22. The Livingston house is sleek and has more elegant touches. *Courtesy of the Burton Historical Collection, Detroit Public Library*

A few years after the restoration of his friend's house, Joy became manager of Packard Motor Company, an automobile manufacturer that was planning to build factories in Detroit. Joy called on Albert to discuss the building of factories, and he ended up hiring Albert to design the Packard Plant on East Grand Boulevard. One of the buildings Albert was to design for the Packard Motor Company proved innovative—a new and improved type of factory building that helped change the ways factories would be designed and built all over the world from then on. Then, a few years later, Joy hired Albert to design a new, large house. What began as a simple restoration project for a friend of Joy's came to have a much greater impact on Albert's professional life. It just goes to show you: small opportunities can quickly grow into large ones.

The second important assignment came during the spring of 1893, and its significance was personal. Albert was contracted to design a house for the Krolik family, who were involved in the dry goods business. Here, a little luck came into play. As Albert met with the family to discuss what they wanted in the house, he became smitten with the family's oldest daughter, Ernestine. She had recently graduated from the University of Michigan, where she studied art, and she was home for the summer. If it had been one season earlier or later, they might not have met.

Ernestine took a great interest in the design of the house, and she asked many questions that Albert was always ready to answer. When she spoke about other things, like art, Albert felt a little shy. Once he began talking about his experiences and his travels in Europe, though, he fascinated her as much as she fascinated him. Albert spent a lot of time on the Krolik project on Adelaide Street in Detroit.

Ernestine and Albert became friends. Though very different, they complemented one another well. He was all business and purpose; she had a flair for noticing things of beauty. Where Albert could make a home sturdy, she could make a room charming. She was interested in arts and literature, and Albert learned much from talking to her. In turn, she learned much from him about architecture and music.

As his friendship with Ernestine grew, Albert learned how to relax—a little. He and Ernestine went to concerts, the theater, and on picnics. On picnics he would sketch the surrounding landscape, and she would read books by famous authors of the time. She liked the novels of English writer George Eliot—an independent and progressive woman, like Ernestine.

Soon they became engaged. But Ernestine went away the next summer to spend a long vacation with her family as their new house was being completed. Albert felt miserable without her. When he wrote letters to her he didn't talk about business, but about crowds on Woodward Avenue—the excitement of the city, and the beautiful summer. He wrote about spending hours in the Detroit Public Library branch downtown on Woodward at Clifford Street reading *The Life of H. H. Richardson*, a famous architect. "How I do wish," he wrote to Ernestine, "that I were a Richardson." Henry Hobson Richardson (1848–1886) had designed churches, libraries, and office buildings with styles that would also show in Albert Kahn's work. Richardson had been impressed by the same kind of architecture that Albert had sketched and become familiar with during his European tour

Albert wrote Ernestine a letter during a trip to New York, where he was designing an estate. He described a visit to Niagara Falls where he found a spot to view the magnificent falls that was away from crowds of tourists. He wrote about the contrast of the power of the waterfalls and the serenity of the surrounding landscape. "This roaring current, and right above it the calmest, quietest, bluest sky one would wish to see," he wrote.

Meanwhile, Albert's reputation as a fine young architect was beginning to spread. He was offered a position in Chicago, Illinois, at the firm of Adler and Sullivan. Louis Sullivan was a famous architect, and Dankmar Adler had once studied drawing in Detroit with Julius Melchers. Adler and Sullivan needed someone to replace another great young architect, Frank Lloyd Wright, who had left to work on his own. But Albert decided to remain in Detroit for several reasons: his family still needed his help; he felt loyal to Mr. Mason; and he wanted to settle down with Ernestine.

Albert and Ernestine were engaged in 1894, one year after they had met. The Krolik family traveled during much of 1895. On September 14, 1896, Albert and Ernestine were married.

1896 was a grand year for Albert for another reason. That year he formed a company of his own with two partners, George Nettleton and Alexander Trowbridge. All three men held important positions with Mason & Rice. There was much architectural work available in the Detroit area and beyond, and the three ambitious young men were ready to run their own company. Their firm, called Nettleton, Kahn, and Trowbridge, opened for business on January 4, 1896. Later that year there would be another important event: an automobile (called a horseless carriage in those days) was driven on a Detroit street for the first time.

Albert's friendship with Mr. Mason was not threatened by the new business venture. There was plenty of work available, and Mr. Mason even helped send some clients to Albert during periods when Mason & Rice had too much work to handle and Albert had none. Mr. Mason knew that starting a new business was difficult: long ago he had started the same way—with ambition, a good reputation, the need to prove himself on his own, and the courage to try.

There were more than the usual ups and downs for the new business. It began in hard economic times. During the period from 1893 to 1897 many people were out of work in Detroit and around the United States, and many businesses failed. But Nettleton, Kahn, and Trowbridge survived. The firm received a commission to design Children's Hospital in Detroit. Another major project came from James Scripps, president of the *Detroit News*. In 1898, Scripps commissioned Albert to design a library and an art gallery next to the Scripps mansion on Trumbull Avenue.

The mansion had elements of English Gothic architecture similar to Westminster Abbey, which Albert had sketched while he was in London. Scripps had a large collection of works by Dutch and Flemish artists, and Albert designed the

Work on the Scripps Library and Museum, built on Trumbull Avenue at Grand River Avenue, reunited Albert with Julius Melchers. The inside of the Scripps Museum, pictured, features a vaulted ceiling. *Courtesy of Cranbrook Archives*

library and museum with slight touches of Flemish architecture he had sketched in Belgium, careful to use similarities in the English and Flemish styles.

His design called for some elaborately sculptured masonry in the Flemish style to decorate the outside of the building. A friend of Mr. Scripps and an old friend of Albert's—Julius Melchers, now in his seventies—was called on to help. Melchers sculpted ornaments from designs Albert drew on paper.

Meanwhile, the firm faced new challenges. One of Albert's partners, Mr. Trowbridge, was offered a position at Cornell University, the college where he and Mr. Nettleton had graduated. He took the position in 1897. Meanwhile, Mr. Nettleton developed health problems and died in 1900.

The firm managed to struggle along, hiring as many good designers as it could afford and stressing teamwork. With Albert's experience, the firm could handle almost any kind of project. Albert began to rely on Ernest Wilby, a young designer who came from Canada to work in Detroit.

When Mr. Nettleton died, Albert had a tough decision to make: Should he play it safe and join another company, or should he dare to go out on his own? On the one hand, he was 31 and was beginning a family with Ernestine—he needed a steady income. On the other hand, Detroit was attracting new businesses and growing in population, and Albert had lots of contacts for possible commissions. Besides, Albert was used to working hard.

The decision was delayed for a few months when Albert and George Mason joined forces to design the Palms Apartment building, which still stands on Jefferson Avenue at the corner of Rivard. For this design they chose elements of architecture from England, which Albert was familiar with from his sketches there. Each corner of the building features six-sided bays, and a balustrade lines the rooftop. For this building Mason and Kahn used a new kind of material—reinforced concrete—for the floors. In this material, steel bars are encased in a mix of concrete; as the concrete dries in a mold it becomes sturdier than other forms of concrete—able to hold more weight—because of the steel bars.

The Palms Apartment building marked the first time that Albert worked with reinforced concrete. Built in 1901, the Palms is east of the Renaissance Center on Jefferson Avenue in Detroit. *Courtesy of Manitou Wordworks*

After the Palms Apartments, Albert was ready for the dare: in 1901, he founded his own architectural firm. It was called ALBERT KAHN, ARCHITECT, ERNEST WILBY, ASSOCIATE.

◆ 5 ◆

"Mr. Kahn,
Can You Design . . . Factories?"

Albert's business was kept very busy from the beginning. Among the firm's first commissions was Albert's first industrial design. In 1901, Joseph Boyer hired Albert to design a factory for Boyer's pneumatic tool company. Pneumatic tools and machines use air pressure to operate. In 1905, Boyer hired Albert to design the Burroughs Adding Machine Company, where the most advanced calculators were manufactured. Both buildings were located on Second Avenue in Detroit.

At first, Albert handled all business negotiations, designs, and office management. Soon, however, there were so many projects that he hired other people to help with the management and work. Among his staff was Ernest Wilby, who served as chief designer, and Albert's brother Julius Kahn, who returned to Detroit in 1902 from Japan, where he had been working. Julius was immediately put to work on a Kahn project that would have great professional significance, as well as personal importance.

After graduating from the Engineering School at the University of Michigan in 1896, Julius became an engineer with the United States Navy, and then with the U.S. Engineering Corps. In 1900 he accepted a position in Japan overseeing the construction and maintenance of iron and sulfur mines.

At the time Julius returned to Detroit, Albert had recently completed Temple Beth El, a synagogue on Woodward Avenue

The School of Engineering building on the campus of the University of Michigan in Ann Arbor. *Bentley Historical Library, University of Michigan*

that is now the Bonstelle Theatre. He also designed the conservatory and the aquarium on Belle Isle. A glass-domed structure housing a collection of plants from around the world, the conservatory is typical of Kahn's designs in its concern for natural lighting. The next project for the firm of Albert Kahn, Architect, Ernest Wilby, Associate, was a new School of Engineering building at the University of Michigan.

Julius found himself back on the campus, but now he was a professional, working for his brother's firm. His specialty as an engineer was arranging tests to determine whether or not construction materials for new buildings were strong enough to support the structure. Albert and Julius wanted to use reinforced concrete for the floors of the Engineering building.

Albert first used that building material in the Palms Apartments project, and Julius was familiar with it from his work with the U.S. Corps of Engineers.

Concrete is made by mixing cement, water, and fine and coarse aggregates. Fine aggregates include material such as sand, and coarse aggregates are materials such as gravel, crushed stone, or slag. The mixture is poured into a mold, much like cake batter poured into a baking pan, where it gradually hardens into the shape of the mold. Reinforced concrete is made by placing metal bars in the mold before pouring in the concrete mix. As the concrete hardens, the bars are encased within. The metal bars make the slab of concrete sturdier and able to support more weight.

However, sometimes the bars move within the hardened concrete if there is even the tiniest bit of space in which to shift. When this occurs, the concrete loses strength and can break. Julius experimented with reinforced concrete and discovered that if the metal bars were bent back, then placed in the concrete mixture, the bars would not move after the concrete hardened. His invention made for a better kind of reinforced concrete. Julius patented the invention, calling it "the Kahn Bar."

Soon after, Julius started a whole separate business where he manufactured reinforcing bars for concrete and other building materials. He formed the Trussed Concrete Steel Company and located the headquarters in Youngstown, Ohio, in the heart of steel manufacturing counties of eastern Ohio and western Pennsylvania.

One day in 1902, as work on the Engineering Building neared completion, Julius came running into Albert's office. "Albert, Henry Joy is here to see you!," he said. "He has an exciting proposal for you!," he continued, as Henry Joy entered the office.

"Mr. Kahn," said Joy, "we haven't met, but I feel like I know you. About ten years ago you designed restoration work on the house of a friend of mine. And another friend of mine,

Joseph Boyer, praises the factory you built for his company. I've been in the home and the factory several times and am very impressed."

Joy explained that he was president of the Packard Motor Car Company, then located in Warren, Ohio. "Packard wants to build factories in Detroit," said Joy. "This is the heart of the automobile industry." Ransome Olds had built the first automobile plant in Detroit in 1899, and Henry Ford started his company in 1903. The Detroit area already had steel plants, railroad car manufacturing facilities, and was a major port for the Great Lakes. As a port city, Detroit grew prosperous during the Civil War (1861–1865), when copper from Michigan was used in the manufacture of weapons. After the war, Michigan was a major source of lumber for houses and furniture throughout the midwest. As a major port and railway center, Detroit had grown into an important city. Mr. Joy's father, James Joy, was a wealthy railroad owner. There were many wealthy people interested in investing money in the new industry of automobile manufacturing.

Joy continued: "Old factory buildings are not suited for new production techniques. We need something newer and better, where workers have more space and can produce cars faster."

Albert hesitated. "I don't have much experience building factories."

"No, but Joseph Boyer recommended you, and I understand you're doing excellent work on the new Engineering Building at the University of Michigan. I am sure you are the man for the job."

"I thank you for your trust in my abilities," said Albert. He reached for paper with one hand and reached for a pencil with the other. Ideas were coming into his mind and he wanted to sketch them out on the drawing board. "Let me draw up some sketches and I will call on you a week from now."

"Wonderful!" exclaimed Mr. Joy. After explaining more of what he needed for his new factory, Henry Joy left the architect to draw up plans. Julius exited the room as well. He knew that Albert would want time to get some of his ideas on paper.

Little did Albert know that this job would launch his reputation as a world-famous factory designer. He would eventually design more than forty buildings for Mr. Joy's Packard company, beginning in 1903.

Factory buildings at that time were cramped and required thick walls and many columns running from the floor up to the ceiling to support the floors and roof above. Parts of floors, walls, and columns were often made of wood, and they easily became fire hazards when oil and grease soaked in. Albert used that style in the first nine buildings he designed for the Packard Motor Company. The tenth building, however, would change the way a modern factory is designed.

Albert was not satisfied with his progress on Joy's ideas. As he began preparing the tenth building, he approached the design like a problem that needs to be solved. The problem: how can he create more inside space by having fewer support columns?

"What we need is a large, open space, where the workers will be comfortable," Albert explained to Julius. "We need to support the weight of the building without dozens of bulky columns running from the ceiling to the floor. We need to provide enough space for many people to work in a single area. And we also need to find ways to let in sunlight and fresh air."

A concrete structure using steel reinforcement was the solution. Because it could support a tremendous amount of weight without cracking, Albert could draw up plans that included fewer columns. With strong, reinforced concrete, walls could have windows that ran from the floor to the ceiling and could be opened to help cool the workplace on warm days.

"If the workers are comfortable, they will work better," Albert explained when presenting Henry Joy the final plans for building #10. "By using concrete for the factory floors, the danger of fire is greatly reduced. There is more space to move about and to do things differently."

Joy was pleased. "I knew you were the right man for the job," he told Albert.

About twenty years later, Albert was interviewed for a feature article in the *Detroit Times* newspaper. He recalled his

Packard Building #10 changed the way factories are designed. By using sturdy, reinforced concrete, Albert was able to design large buildings with many windows. Inside, the reinforced concrete required fewer support columns, giving workers more room to move and build. *Albert Kahn Associates, Inc., Architects & Engineers*

Packard factory design: "To every man there comes one BIG opportunity. He should be prepared when that golden chance in his life comes along. My chance came when Mr. Joy commissioned me to design the first Packard plant here in Detroit."

Albert approached the design of the Packard plant with the same philosophy he used in all of his designs. Albert felt the outward appearance of a building should reflect the activities housed within: his factories were large and sturdy, and his houses were roomy, secure, and inviting. All of his buildings featured many windows to let in as much daylight as possible, even the factories. Albert believed that the environment around you has a strong influence on your life and your work, and he wanted to make his buildings as pleasant and useful as possible.

The Packard Building #10, on East Grand Boulevard between Packard and Concord, was one of the first American factories built with reinforced concrete. Albert had no handbook to use. Through his work, a new material and a new design concept were combined to form a new kind of building. Unlike the dark and cramped mills of the past, the modern factory would have open space and plenty of daylight.

"You know," he told Julius as they walked around the completed Packard Building #10, "when I began as an architect, the real architects would design only museums, cathedrals, capitals, and monuments. The office boy was considered good enough to do factories." Albert smiled at Julius and concluded, "I'm still that office boy designing factories. I have no 'dignity' to be impaired." He meant that he wasn't too proud to perform less glamorous work. That modesty had allowed him to seize an opportunity others might have scorned—and ultimately made him one of the most famous American architects in history.

After the Packard plant was completed, Albert was approached by other automobile manufacturers asking him to design their factories. In addition to designing other factories for the booming Detroit automobile industry, Albert designed the Pierce-Arrow automobile plant in Buffalo, New York.

Meanwhile, a new approach for making cars more quickly and more affordably was brewing in the mind of another auto pioneer, Henry Ford. Ford's ideas began to take shape when he realized that the two factories he had were not sufficient to increase production.

Ford had big plans for making automobiles available to the general public. At the time, most cars were expensive and hard to operate. Ford was planning to introduce the Model T— a car that was simple to operate and inexpensive to buy. He wanted to build more Model Ts in one year than all the other kinds of cars that were built around the world combined. He had many bold ideas.

"Mr. Kahn, can you design more efficient factories?" Henry Ford asked over the telephone. Ford liked to get right to the point.

"Mr. Ford, I can design anything," was Albert's reply. He now had confidence, since having designed Joy's plant.

They met a week later in Ford's office at his factory on Piquette Avenue in Detroit.

They drove up Woodward Avenue from the factory. "I want to make a car that can be inexpensive, easy to use, and produced in large quantities," explained Ford during the ride, referring to what would become known as the Model T. "I plan to have the entire car built under one roof, from start to finish. I want to build a factory on property I own," Mr. Ford told the architect. They toured the large piece of vacant land Ford owned in Highland Park, at the time a small, rural area outside of the city of Detroit.

"Impossible," Albert thought. He had designed many buildings for Packard. Even with his sleek designs for automobile factories, production would have to take place in more than one building. Still, he was intrigued. After Kahn and Ford returned to Ford's office, Albert sharpened a pencil and began to draw a rough sketch, placing the proposed building in the middle of his outline of Mr. Ford's 230-acre property.

"You've only got part of the idea," Mr. Ford interrupted. "I want the first building constructed right up along Woodward Avenue so that I have room to expand behind, to other parts of the property." Ford continued: "This factory will take us into the future. Everything will be geared toward building cars faster. Each worker will perform only one task, with all the parts and tools they need right by their side. Someday, instead of having workers move around to stations, we will have a moving assembly line that will bring work to the workers."

Albert took another pencil and wrote notes on another piece of paper. When listening to clients he would use one pencil to sketch ideas and another to make notes. He wanted to be sure he knew exactly what the client wanted. He believed, as he often told his staff, "The client's analysis of a problem is the first step toward solution." Because he listened much more than he spoke, Albert seemed modest to many people. He simply believed that you learn more by listening than by talking.

Ford's ideas seemed wild to Albert. But he knew that Henry Ford was a determined man and an inventor filled with hope for progress through industrialization and technology. Besides, until Ford's ideas proved impractical to design, Albert felt he had to try to solve the problem of building even larger factories with better working environments.

After dinner that evening, Albert went straight to his office on Wayne Street near the corner of Lafayette Avenue (an area that was later changed significantly when Washington Boulevard was expanded). He worked late into the night on design plans, except for a short nap where the plans swirled around in his dreams. He awoke and completed a rough outline of plans as the first rays of morning filtered in through the office curtains.

Albert packed his work up. After talking about the project with Ernest Wilby when he arrived for work, Albert left the office. He walked east on Lafayette Avenue to Woodward Avenue, where he caught a streetcar to take him to his new home on Mack Avenue.

He had already planned for two rare vacation days. That afternoon, he and Ernestine were going to a Detroit Tigers baseball game. The Tigers were playing in the World Series against the Chicago Cubs. The next day, the entire family— Albert and Ernestine and their four children—were going to take the streetcar down Woodward Avenue to the riverside, where they would take a ferry to Belle Isle and have a picnic. The children would enjoy riding on the ferry more than taking a streetcar down Jefferson Avenue to the wooden bridge that connected to Belle Isle. Families would go to Belle Isle just as they do today, for picnics, to canoe the streams and small lakes, play games, and tour the conservatory.

That day, after Albert took a nap and ate breakfast, he and Ernestine rode a streetcar down Woodward to Michigan Avenue and then took another streetcar west to the ballpark at

The Ford Highland Park Plant, where Model Ts were built. The factory building was nicknamed the Crystal Palace because of its many windows (most of which have awnings in this rare photograph from 1913). The Administration Building, where Henry Ford had an office, is on the left. Further left is the Power House with its distinctive five huge smokestacks. *From the collections of Henry Ford Museum and Greenfield Village*

the intersection of Michigan and Trumbull. At the time, the Tigers' ballpark was called Bennett Park. The baseball diamond was built right on top of the cobblestones used to pave an old hay market, and bleachers held as many as ten thousand fans. The Detroit Tigers had played there as part of the American League since it began operation in 1901. The Tigers had never won much before, but now they were playing in the World Series. They had an exciting young outfielder named Ty Cobb, who, as a twenty-year-old rookie, was the leading hitter in the league. Playing next to him in the outfield was another great hitter, "Wahoo" Sam Crawford.

As Albert and Ernestine rode to the ballpark, Albert talked with his wife about the Ford project. A streetcar passed heading the other way, and someone shouted, "Ee-Yah!" Several other people responded, "Ee-Yah!" That was the Tigers's rallying cry. Manager Hughie Jennings yelled it out during ball games to encourage fans to cheer more loudly for the team. Now the cry was often heard on the city streets.

"I think he's crazy," said Albert.

"Oh, he's just an excited fan," replied Ernestine.

"No, I mean Henry Ford. I don't think it's possible to have all production stages under one roof. But I didn't want to tell him that." Looking around the streetcar, he wondered how different the future would be if even half of the riders were able to drive cars instead.

"You've always risen to challenges before," said Ernestine.

"Never one this big," replied Albert. As he repeated the phrase, the project began to seem more and more like a problem that needed to be solved on the drawing board. "I have to try. I want to see what can be done. It takes a live fish to swim upstream," he mumbled to himself.

The Tigers lost the World Series that year as part of a three-year World Series losing streak—1907 through 1909. But win or lose, baseball became a permanent part of life in Detroit. So did automobiles, as Albert designed the factory that Henry Ford needed to try out his new idea—the Model T.

Ford Motor Company's Highland Park Automobile Assembly Building opened on New Year's Day 1910. Designed by Albert Kahn, the factory was almost as long as three football fields and stood four stories tall. The factory earned the nickname "The Crystal Palace" because its windows, which ran along the side of every floor and parts of the roof, glistened in the sunlight and provided great light for the work going on inside. The building's large open space allowed all production to take place under one roof.

Even though Albert had designed a massive and innovative building, it proved to be adaptable to further innovation. The open space of the Highland Park plant was adapted a couple of years later when Henry Ford introduced the automobile assembly line. It allowed for the assembly of a car to progress to different areas, where different parts were stored. That would have been impossible in the old mills, where many columns interfered with free movement.

Inside the Crystal Palace, beneath a roof of glass (or "monitors" in architectural terms). In the Ford Highland Park Plant, work progressed from the top floor to ground level. When workers finished assembling parts, the parts were placed in bins that moved downward to the next floor, where more parts were added. Cars were completed on the ground floor and driven out of the plant to a garage. *Albert Kahn Associates, Inc., Architects & Engineers*

In all, Albert designed several other buildings for Mr. Ford's Highland Park complex, including a machine shop with skylights to let in sunlight and air, and a power house with five huge smoke stacks. He also added on to the Crystal Palace to speed up production even more. Mr. Ford moved his offices from Woodward and Grand Boulevard in Detroit to the new

Workers testing engines inside the Ford Highland Park Plant before the motors were added to automobiles-in-progress. *From the collections of Henry Ford Museum and Greenfield Village*

Administration Building in Highland Park that Albert and Ernest Wilby had designed. That building still stands on Woodward Avenue, with a historical marker in front.

Albert had helped Henry Ford realize his vision of the assembly line, which resulted in a great increase in car production and helped make more cars available to the general public. Back in 1904, for example, 22,000 cars were manufactured in the whole world. In 1914, a year after Henry Ford introduced his assembly line, the Ford Motor Company alone produced 248,307 Model Ts!

A completed Eagle Boat, or "submarine chaser," emerges from the Ford Rouge Plant in 1919. This was the last boat produced at the factory. World War I had recently ended. The factory was then transformed for a peacetime activity—manufacturing automobiles. *From the collections of Henry Ford Museum and Greenfield Village*

Workers came to the Detroit area from all over for jobs in the auto industry. Over thirty different languages were spoken by workers at the Highland Park plant. During the period from 1913 to 1918, almost half a million African Americans left their farm life to work and live in cities like Detroit.

By 1915, Ford Motor Company was making so many cars that the Highland Park facility was becoming too small. Ford

An Eagle Boat at sea. *From the collections of Henry Ford Museum and Greenfield Village*

called on Albert again after acquiring 2,000 acres of land along the Rouge River, near to where it empties into the Detroit River.

"Albert," Mr. Ford said to the architect, "I need you to design a new factory. This time, I want all production, from start to finish, to take place not just under the same roof, but on the same floor." Ford also wanted the plant to be entirely self-sufficient, from making steel and glass to assembling cars. Albert welcomed these challenges.

World War I was raging in Europe at that time. The half-mile-long B Building at Henry Ford's new site on the Rouge River in Dearborn was first used in 1917 to build Eagle Boat "submarine chasers" for use in World War I. There had to be enough room to allow for the size of the boats. Previous to the production of boats inside the Rouge plant, almost all boat

Albert Kahn *(far left)* and Henry Ford *(second from left)* observe a demonstration of part of an aiplane engine. *Albert Kahn Associates, Inc., Architects & Engineers*

building throughout history had been done outside. Inside the roomy Rouge plant, boat building could proceed continuously, faster, and more efficiently—in any season of the year.

After World War I ended in 1919, this new factory made of steel and glass was used to build automobiles. Ever resourceful, Albert had used steel instead of reinforced concrete at the Rouge. His designs ensured that the steel beams would be strong enough to form huge structures. The interiors of these large structures could be changed more easily than concrete

The William L. Clements Library on the campus of the University of Michigan. The entrance is a triple-arched portico, in the style of the Italian Renaissance—a design Albert also used for the entrance to the General Motors building. *Bentley Historical Library, University of Michigan*

structures to adapt to different needs and changing times. The Rouge was quickly changed from a boat-building to a car-building facility.

Albert added many other facilities to the Rouge. They included a foundry, where steel for the automobile bodies was made, and a glass factory, where glass for the windows and windshields was formed.

As busy as he was with Mr. Ford, Albert still found time to design houses, buildings for business and recreation, and other structures. Albert designed several more buildings for the University of Michigan, including a hospital, schools, a library, and an auditorium. In all, he designed twenty-six buildings for the University; most of them are still in use today.

A panoramic view of the huge University of Michigan Hospital *(top half of photo)*. *Bentley Historical Library, University of Michigan*

The William L. Clements Library on the campus was based on a villa Albert photographed and sketched in Italy. It is a one-story building that houses rare books and a collection of historical items from American history. The University of Michigan Hospital, on the other hand, is a massive structure.

Hill Auditorium and Angell Hall are among Albert's most artistic designs. Angell Hall, the University's primary class-

Angell Hall—one of twenty-six Kahn-designed buildings on the University of Michigan campus. *Bentley Historical Library, University of Michigan*

room and administrative building, features grand, cylindrical columns running across the front of the building. Many say the building resembles the Lincoln Memorial in Washington, D.C., which was designed by Albert's friend Henry Bacon.

Albert also continued to design private homes. Since the early 1900s, he had become very interested in the Arts and

Crafts movement. Arts and Crafts designs emphasize crafts-manship—objects crafted by humans as opposed to machines, from furniture to architecture. The "cottage style" of architecture of the Arts and Crafts movement emphasized simple shapes and harmony with the natural landscape. It was the style Albert and Ernestine chose for their own home, which they built at the corner of Mack Avenue and John R in Detroit.

The Arts and Crafts movement began in the mid-nineteenth century in Great Britain and the United States. Craft workshops and exhibitions became popular in the 1890s. Albert Kahn drew on the style when he designed the interior of his new home, and the furniture within.

◆ 6 ◆

Work and Play

"It is beautiful!" exclaimed Ernestine Kahn, standing on the steps of her new home. Albert designed the family home for himself, Ernestine, and their four children to resemble the cottages he had seen in the English countryside. Architects in England and the United States at the time were modernizing the English style of cottages, making the shapes plainer and allowing for more window space—typical of the Arts and Crafts movement.

Albert had forbidden her from visiting their new residence during the final few weeks of construction in 1907 while the finishing touches were added to the exterior. He wanted Ernestine to wait and see the house in its full glory.

"I love it," Ernestine enthused.

"Now close your eyes," Albert told his wife. "I have a surprise." He took Ernestine's hand and led her to the back of the house.

"Okay, Ernestine." Albert said. Ernestine opened her eyes and saw a finely landscaped garden, with lilac bushes, rhododendrons, lillies, and roses in every imaginable color. They both took turns looking at each other, the garden, and the new home with great delight. Everything was perfect.

"The garden is more important than the house to me," Albert had told his brother Julius when he was designing the new home. As busy as he would become, Albert would find time to tend to his beautiful garden. "I like to play at landscape gardening," he said. "I believe as much attention should be

65

The Albert Kahn House, built in 1907. The house still stands on Mack Avenue and is used as the office of the Urban League of Detroit. Favoring the style of architecture called Domestic Revival that became popular in Great Britian during the nineteenth century, the design emphasized a simple, massive appearance with many windows, most of which are grouped together. The surrounding landscape of lush vegetation is part of the design. The bay on the front right side provides for more sunlight to illuminate the interior. *Albert Kahn Associates, Inc., Architects & Engineers*

spent on land as on the house in cities." Taking care of his own lot—to make it as useful and beautiful as possible—was Albert's philosophy.

Ten years later, Albert would delight Ernestine and the children again with a full cottage on Walnut Lake in Bloomfield Hills, about 20 miles northwest of their home. The cottage was built in the Prairie style popularized by architect

The Kahn cottage on Walnut Lake, seen from the garden side. There are several things to look for in this photo. Notice the smooth angles of the house—it appears to rise up naturally, as part of the landscape. The cottage also features many windows that catch summer breezes for natural ventilation. Finally, the landscaped garden was important in all of Albert's home designs. *Albert Kahn Associates, Inc., Architects & Engineers*

Frank Lloyd Wright. The Prairie style, like the Arts and Crafts style, emphasized harmony between a building and the surrounding landscape, but favored sleeker, modern styles and materials.

Meanwhile, as Albert's work with Henry Ford became busier and busier, factory designs demanded more and more of his attention. To manage the ever-growing work flow, he developed a regimented production system for the design of buildings—much like Henry Ford's assembly line for cars. This system was aimed at eliminating any wasteful actions, so that Albert Kahn's buildings could be designed as efficiently as

Henry Ford's automobiles were produced. An important part of Albert Kahn's efficient design theory was that he placed as much importance on knowledge of engineering as on knowledge of architecture. Brothers Moritz and Louis joined the firm and were important contributors to realizing that philosophy.

As Albert finished up his designs for the Highland Park Plant and later the Rouge Plant for Mr. Ford, he continued to work on factories for the other founders of the city's automobile industry. Somehow, he also found time to design homes for some of his friends and to design many of the most impressive buildings in Detroit. Police Headquarters on Beaubien Street, the First National Bank Building on Woodward, and many other structures designed by Albert helped transform Detroit into a modern city with architectural features reminiscent of European styles.

While he worked long hours, Albert also placed great importance on spending time with his family and pursuing outside interests. Along with Ernestine, he was active in the Arts and Crafts Society of Detroit, a group that studied and educated the public on this architectural and decorative style. When daughter Lydia wanted a dollhouse, Albert was not satisfied with ones he saw in stores. Instead, he commissioned a friend to design a dollhouse in the Arts and Crafts style, with all the representative features of a real house. He explained that he wanted to help nurture his daughter's artistic taste.

Albert and Ernestine attended concerts of the Detroit Symphony Orchestra and collected fine works of art, some of which were later donated to the Detroit Institute of Arts (DIA). Albert served as Arts commissioner for the DIA, helping select artworks for the museum's collection. In 1927 he recommended Paul P. Cret, a Philadelphia-based architect, to design a new DIA building. The Italian Renaissance-styled Detroit Institute of Arts building on Woodward Avenue, designed by Cret, is an artwork in itself. Albert would eventually add an art gallery onto the Kahn family home.

Summer Sundays were always spent at the cottage at Walnut Lake, where the entire Kahn clan—Albert and his brothers and sisters, their wives and husbands and children—

The Booth House, now known as Cranbrook House, as viewed from the south courtyard. Like Albert's home, pictured on p.66, the Booth House favors a simple design emphasizing many windows. Several terraces overlook extensive gardens. The simple design that harmonizes with nature is an element of the Arts and Crafts style. The wing jutting forward on the right, added later, has the familiar triple-arched opening Albert Kahn used in the Clements library and the General Motors building. *Courtesy of Cranbrook Archives*

gathered for picnics and swimming. It was a long way from his humble beginnings.

Soon after finishing his own home in 1907 and while he was beginning work on the Ford Highland Park plant, Albert designed the Bloomfield Hills residence of his friend George Booth. Mr. Booth owned the *Detroit News*. Albert would later design the newspaper's office building, as well as those of the competing *Detroit Free Press* and *Detroit Times,* in downtown

The General Motors Building in the late 1920s. Both the marble walls and floors on the inside, and the arcade (the series of arches) forming the outside base of the building are elements of Italian Renaissance architecture. *Courtesy of the Burton Historical Collection, Detroit Public Library*

Albert and Ernestine Kahn and some pigeons in the Piazza San
Marco, Venice, Italy, in 1927. *Courtesy of Cranbrook Archives*

Detroit. Mr. Booth was president of the Arts and Crafts Society. Although his home was grand, it incorporated the simplicity of the cottage style of the Arts and Crafts movement. Today, the home is known as the Cranbrook House and is part of the Cranbrook academic community in Bloomfield Hills.

Meanwhile, Henry Joy came back into the picture. He helped Albert secure other important projects like the Detroit Athletic Club building on Madison Street. Mr. Joy was vice-president of the private businessmen's club. Albert and Ernestine had just returned from a trip to Italy and Spain when Albert received the commission for the building in 1912.

"Every architect must have a signature project, a work which he feels best expresses his ideals," Albert told Joy. "The Detroit Athletic Club will be mine." He designed the building in a style known as Renaissance Revival to resemble the monuments he had seen on his recent trip in Italy. The style had been made popular by architects who designed athletic clubs in New York City. Albert had toured some of them during trips to New York.

Albert was invited to join the Detroit Athletic Club, but he declined. He had too much work to do, he told Henry Joy. Also, Albert was bothered that there were no other Jewish members of the club, and none seemed likely to be invited soon. Although he never spoke publicly on the issue, Albert was disturbed by such quiet forms of discrimination as well as the more obvious examples, like those publicized by Henry Ford in Ford-owned newspapers.

The influence of Italian architecture in the Detroit Athletic Club can also be seen in one of Albert's most important designs—the 23-story General Motors Building on Grand Boulevard in Detroit. Arches run all along the base of the building. A series of arches like that—typical of Italian Renaissance architecture—is called an arcade. The use of marble inside the building also provides a flavor of the Renaissance.

At the time it was completed in 1922, the General Motors Building was the second largest office building in the world. Rather than constructing one solid mass or a tall skyscraper,

Panoramic view of the lakeside facade of the Edsel and Eleanor Ford House, designed by Albert to resemble cottages of the Cotswold District in England. Windows, brickwork, lush natural surroundings, and simple shapes are elements of the cottage style. *Courtesy of the Edsel and Eleanor Ford House; photograph by Balthazar Korab*

Albert designed the building with four projecting wings so that every office had a window. He always wanted people to have enough light and space.

"Space and light are important to workers, whether on the factory floor or sitting behind a desk," Albert explained to William Durant, the founder of General Motors.

After Albert completed the General Motors Building, he returned twice again to Europe, including tours in Italy, Spain, France, and England. Outings in the English country-

Eliel Saarinen's design for the Chicago Tribune competition. The design was widely admired for its sleek, modern look and led several American universities to invite Saarinen to teach. Saarinen's design finished second in the competition and was never built. Albert Kahn was inspired by the design, and the Fisher Building bears some resemblance to Saarinen's drawing (see p. 77). *Courtesy of Cranbrook Archives*

side provided the basis for his next non-industrial commission—the Edsel Ford home on Lake St. Clair in Grosse Pointe Shores.

Edsel, Henry Ford's son, had traveled to Europe with his father. They both greatly admired the cottages they saw in the Cotswold district of the English countryside. The architectural style of the cottages is called the Tudor style. Henry Ford had a Tudor-style cottage imported from the Cotswold district and placed in Greenfield Village, the outdoor museum he established near the Rouge plant. Edsel, on the other hand, opted for his own Cotswold cottage, and he asked Albert Kahn to design it for him.

"Spare no expense," he directed Albert. "This will be my family's sanctuary and I want it to be perfect." Albert traveled to England to further study the cottages in the Cotswold district. Not only did he import stones for the roof and fireplace from England, he brought in expert British workmen to lay them!

Later, Albert designed another home in the Tudor style. This one, in Bloomfield Hills, was for James Couzens, who was once an officer at the Ford Motor Company, was elected mayor of Detroit in 1919, and was once a state senator. Kahn became so fond of this style, he used it for the art gallery he designed as an addition to his family's Mack Avenue home.

Albert also admired the designs of Eliel Saarinen, a Finnish architect who came to Ann Arbor to teach at the University of Michigan. Saarinen won much praise for his entry in the Chicago Tribune Competition of 1922—a design contest sponsored by the Chicago Tribune newspaper for its new headquarters. Saarinen's design didn't win—it finished in second place among the contest judges—but it was well-liked by so many architects that he received many invitations to relocate to the United States. The design Saarinen submitted blended historical and modern elements into a clean simplicity that gave the buildings a telescope form, tapering toward the top.

When Saarinen became president of the Cranbrook Academy of Art, he and Albert became friends. Saarinen spent much time at the Kahn's summer home, which was very close to Cranbrook. He and Albert played lawn games, listened to classical music, and discussed architecture as well as Albert's favorite warm-weather diversion—the Detroit Tigers baseball team. Evenings were spent on a porch that was designed to catch summer breezes and overlook the garden. Albert modeled one of his most important buildings—the Fisher Building—after the work of Saarinen, a colleague whom he admired so much.

Commissioned by the seven Fisher brothers, founders of the Fisher Body Corporation, the Fisher Building was planned to house offices, shops, and a grand movie palace. Today that theatre hosts plays and musical productions. Back when it was a movie palace, Albert and Ernestine went there to see films. Albert especially liked the ones starring Charlie Chaplin.

"This will be our signature building," Fred Fisher told Albert; Albert had previously designed a factory in Cleveland, Ohio, for the Fisher brothers. The Fisher family had long been prominent in Detroit. They established a thriving carriage-building business and then adapted the carriage body so it could be motor driven, moving from horse-drawn carriages to "horseless carriages," as automobiles were called in the 1890s. "It is to be the tallest building outside of downtown Detroit," Fred Fisher told Albert. Indeed, the New Center area of Detroit is still identifiable today by the grand tower of the steel-framed and stone-sheathed Fisher Building.

Completed in 1928, the building is marked by elegant decorative touches. Entering the building through an arched entrance one sees an interior arcade, an arched ceiling, large windows looking over the street on either end, and intricate ironwork. Recesses in the tall facade—the face of the building—allow for many sets of windows within the massive concrete structure, and the building tapers in toward the top. The patterns of bright color inside the building are characteristic of the Arts and Crafts movement.

The Fisher Building was honored as 1928's most beautiful commercial structure by the Architecture League of New York. Like his commission for the Edsel Ford House, Albert was given a large budget to work with. The Fisher Brothers had

The Fisher Building, right across the street from the General Motors building. It was honored as the year's most beautiful commercial structure by the Architecture League of New York in 1928 and is considered Detroit's largest piece of art. The main floor arcade features elaborate marble work and houses shops and a theatre. The stone exterior features a series of recesses from side to side while the building tapers as it rises to the main tower. *Albert Kahn Associates, Inc., Architects & Engineers*

made a fortune by perfecting the closed-body car—an improvement on the open-air seating of early automobiles. The large budget allowed Albert to find new ways to express elegance without being showy. The Fisher Building is often called Detroit's largest work of art.

Both the Fisher Building and the Edsel Ford house were designed and built during a time of great economic prosperity in America—the era known as "The Roaring 20s." Detroit boomed during the 1920s. At the start of the decade it was the ninth largest city in the United States. At the end of the decade, it was the fourth largest. Soon, however, those boom times went bust throughout the United States with the Great Depression of the 1930s and the horrors of a world at war, beginning in 1939. The bad economic times made it impossible to complete the entire Fisher Building plans. For the famous 28-story Fisher Building was originally designed to have a twin 28-story tower. These twin towers were supposed to form the corners of a large complex that would have a giant, 42-story tower in the middle. But the plans were never completed.

There was other work to do. Albert Kahn's firm managed to remain strong through the Great Depression years. The firm helped improve conditions in economic hard times and later helped design factories that built the supplies used by the American military in World War II.

◆ 7 ◆

The Great Depression and War Years

More than a year after the Fisher Building was completed, a delegation of engineers and officials from the Soviet Union toured the United States. Russia, the largest republic of the Soviet Union, had suffered great damage during World War I, which ended almost ten years earlier. The country had been slow to modernize and needed help to establish industries that employed people. Workers would build the tractors and farm equipment needed to harvest crops and the heavy machinery needed to build roads, houses, buildings, and cities.

When the delegation stopped in Detroit, Albert was invited to meet them at a reception.

"We have visited many grand buildings in your city," a man called Comrade Petrovic, the leader of the delegation, said to Albert at the reception. "Every time we asked who designed this great building or that great building, we were given the same name: Albert Kahn."

Albert knew that the United States government was interested in helping the Soviet Union to modernize, for humanitarian and economic reasons. Even Henry Ford, an ardent anti-communist, agreed that sharing the benefits of industrial progress was a good thing.

"Factories and businesses in Russia are not as advanced as those in your country," continued Comrade Petrovic to Albert. "Many of the products we need, like cars for transportation, and tractors for our farms, we have to buy from other countries. We have asked the American government to help us pro-

Inside the Tractor Plant at Chelyabinsk, Russia, in 1933. This plant was one of over five hundred factories in Russia designed by Albert Kahn Associates. *Albert Kahn Associates, Inc., Architects & Engineers*

vide work and products for the Soviet people. We wish to create more jobs in manufacturing, such as the production of automobiles, and technology, and electronic devices. We want to talk with you about designing the buildings for this work."

A few days later, Moritz, Louis and other staff members at Albert Kahn Associates were standing around a drafting table. Moritz was reading aloud an article from the *New York Times*. The date was May 7, 1929. "American to Build Soviet Auto Plants," announced the headline, and the article began:

> Albert Kahn, architect, of Detroit, has been engaged by
> the Soviet Government to plan and supervise the construc-
> tion of a large group of manufacturing plants at Stalingrad,
> at the mouth of the Volga River, in Russia, it was made
> known yesterday.

Albert, of course, missed out on all the excitement. He was in his office, shirtsleeves rolled to his elbows, working on a new design for Mr. Ford before moving on to another historic industrial project.

Albert Kahn Associates set up an office in Moscow, headed by Moritz Kahn. The partnership with the Russian government lasted only four years, but in that time the 30 Russian and American employees of the Kahn and Associates' Moscow office supervised the design of more than 500 buildings. Under Moritz's direction, the architects, engineers and technicians created steel, automobile, and tractor factories, and airplane and chemical plants. Moritz was in close contact with his brother about all the projects. The tractor factory in Stalingrad (now named Volgograd) was an especially great triumph, employing many new workers to build the machinery necessary to modernize Russian agriculture.

To design so many buildings so quickly, over 1,500 Soviet draftsmen were employed. They worked by day and attended classes at night to learn the techniques of Albert Kahn Associates. New architects were being taught, many construction workers found work building the factories, and many workers were employed in the factories building the machinery needed to modernize Soviet agriculture.

The impact of Albert Kahn's buildings on the Russian way of life was truly significant. Years later, Soviet architect Viktor A. Vesnin wrote a letter to Ernestine Kahn. Albert, he wrote, "rendered us great service in designing a number of large plants and helped us to assimilate to the American experience in the sphere of the building industry. Soviet engineers and architects will always warmly remember the name of talented American engineer and architect, Albert Kahn."

America was beginning its own hard times during the period when Albert Kahn Associates was helping the Soviet

Union. The Great Depression lasted throughout the 1930s, and many people were out of work. The Soviet commission allowed Albert Kahn Associates to continue to employ a full staff.

Meanwhile, Albert continued his industrial work and also designed a pavilion for Ford for the 1932 Chicago World's Fair. The World's Fair was an event that occurred every four years in different cities all over the world and lasted for an entire year. It featured exhibitions of new technologies, products, designs and ideas in many fields, from automobile production to gardening. The pavilions housing those exhibitions were elaborate and constructed just as carefully as any building intended for everyday use. Many pavilions were put into everyday use following the fair. The Ford Rotunda Building, which housed an exhibit on the history of transportation, was disassembled after the fair, moved to Dearborn, and became part of the Ford Motor Company's Rouge complex. Kahn later helped design the pavilions for both Ford and General Motors at the 1939 New York World's Fair.

In 1936, Albert designed a steel mill for the Republic Steel Corporation in Cleveland, Ohio. This marked the first time in history an American steel company commissioned an outside architect, rather than one of its own engineers, to design a factory. The Kahn family had a connection with Republic Steel: Republic had purchased Julius Kahn's Trussed Concrete Steel Company several years earlier.

Albert continued his work for Henry Ford, adding a tire factory to the Rouge complex. Around the same time, he designed two important buildings for the Chrysler Corporation. Both the De Soto Press Shop, built at the corner of McGraw and Wyoming avenues in Detroit, and the Half-Ton Truck Plant, at Mound and Eight Mile roads in Warren, with their box-shaped, steel-framed designs and walls made completely of glass, were praised for their simplicity and innovation. The two buildings were featured in the August 1938 issue of the important journal, *Architectural Forum*. The entire issue was dedicated to Albert's work.

The Half-Ton Truck Plant was considered so sleekly modern and well-lit that pictures of it were displayed in an exhibi-

Albert working at his desk at home in 1931. *Walter P. Reuther Library, Wayne State University*

tion of modern architecture at New York's Museum of Modern Art in 1944. It was described as a steel skeleton with glass skin brightened and warmed by sunlight.

As Albert completed those projects, the political climate in America, and the world, was drastically changing. World War II broke out in Europe in 1939. In 1941, the United States entered the war. America's demand for cars turned to a need for tanks and war planes. With its many factories and industrial workers, Detroit became the center for war-time industry. Many of the same materials for building cars were used to build defense vehicles, and workers made everything from helmets to tanks. Detroit became known as the Arsenal of Democracy. All the automobile companies used their resources to build weapons and war vehicles, and they turned to the same architect they had always relied upon to design their factories—Albert Kahn.

Business had always moved briskly at Albert Kahn Associates. By 1938, one of every five industrial plants throughout the United States was designed by Albert Kahn Associates. During wartime the pace picked up even more. Albert increased his staff of 400 to 600 architects, engineers and technicians, many of whom worked around the clock on various projects. It was not uncommon for Albert to spend his short nights sleeping in the office, with his head on his drafting table! "Speed, and more speed!" became the motto at the firm to design the factories that manufactured the supplies needed for the war effort.

One of Albert's most important projects during World War II was the Chrysler Corporation Tank Arsenal. Built in 1941 on 113 acres of farmland in Warren, it was the first heavy tank plant built in America. Its long glass walls were often compared to those of the B Building at the Ford Rouge plant. The tanks produced at the Arsenal were credited with winning important battles in North Africa during the war—Sir Winston Churchill himself, the British Prime Minister, later credited the tanks built in Warren for the breakthrough in the war against German forces in North Africa.

During World War II, Henry Ford called upon Albert to design an airplane bomber plant at Willow Run, near Ann Arbor. The assembly line at the Willow Run Bomber Plant extended 3000 feet, with raw materials delivered on one end and finished planes emerging on the other. Then, the planes were flown away using a runway next to the plant. Over 8,000 B-24 Bombers were manufactured at Willow Run during World War II.

Inside the Chrysler Corporation Tank Arsenal with an example of its output for use in World War II. The tanks produced at this facility helped defeat Nazi forces in North Africa around the time that Albert Kahn died. *Albert Kahn Associates, Inc., Architects & Engineers*

More than 50,000 workers were needed to work at Willow Run. The first expressway in Michigan was built from Detroit to an area near the plant so workers could drive to the plant. The expressway opened in September of 1942.

Because of the need to prepare for wartime blackouts, when lights had to be extinguished in factories in case enemy planes might attack, Albert provided for no windows. Instead, the factory had artificial light. Thus, for the first and only time, he abandoned his standard practice of providing workers with maximum daylight to work in.

For awhile, the Willow Run plant was the largest war factory in the world. That distinction changed when Albert designed the Dodge Machine & Assembly Building in Chicago, Illinois, financed by the U.S. Department of Defense. Because the use of steel was restricted by the government for other military purposes, Albert had to change his original design to account for a cement roof that would weigh twice as much as his originally planned steel-supported roof. Albert successfully solved the problem of creating this massive roof by using arches. He remarked that long ago, in the days before steel was manufactured, famous Renaissance artist and architect Leonardo da Vinci had used arch construction for his buildings "because he had no steel to work with," and added: "We are using (arch construction) because we haven't very much (steel)."

That huge structure would later be transformed into a shopping mall. In fact, many Albert Kahn-designed buildings were later used for other purposes. In Harbortown on Detroit's riverfront, for example, a building originally used for manufacturing for the large Parke-Davis pharmacy company was transformed into part of what is now Stroh River Place, with shops, offices, large apartments, and restaurants. Albert's buildings weren't just functional, they were multi-functional!

During World War II, planes and tanks built in Albert Kahn-designed factories helped win many important battles. Planes flying missions in the Pacific region took off and landed at air force bases on such islands as Hawaii and Midway. These bases were also designed by Albert Kahn Associates.

The factories and bases were important, large-scale, and fast-paced projects. When the war started, Albert was already seventy years old. At a time when he might look forward to rest, especially after having suffered two heart attacks, Albert continued his important work. In November 1942, he suffered a third heart attack, complicated by a bronchial ailment. Even this illness, very severe at that time, couldn't stop Albert from drawing new buildings. He continued to review designs for new factories from his bed, covered with quilts and blueprints.

On December 8, 1942, after setting aside the blueprints, he stopped working. Albert invited his daughter Rosalie into the room and wished her a happy birthday. Rosalie, near forty, was visiting her ailing father. After they visited, Albert tried to go back to the blueprints lying around his bed, but he couldn't work any longer. Ernestine was at his side. "I just want to rest," he told her.

Albert Kahn had worked countless hours a day nearly every day since he was twelve. He closed his eyes and reflected on the good life he had lived: his buildings had changed Detroit, America, and the world. And even though he worked tirelessly, he had enjoyed many symphonies, times in the garden, Tiger games, and Sundays at Walnut Lake, with Ernestine, his children, and his dear friends. Thinking of all this peacefully, Albert Kahn passed away.

EPILOGUE

Albert Kahn's funeral was held at Temple Beth El, a synagogue on Woodward Avenue in Detroit that he himself designed and which was built in 1927. It features massive columns that rise above stairs and evokes a sense of awe and reverence in a portico before the temple doorway. An earlier Temple Beth El, that he designed and built in 1903, has only hints of its original design but is still in use as Wayne State University's Bonstelle Theatre.

Outside the temple after the funeral, a *Detroit News* reporter interviewed Henry Ford.

"What are your memories of Albert Kahn?" the reporter asked. At the time of his death, Albert had designed over one thousand buildings for Mr. Ford alone. In all, Albert Kahn-designed structures are located in 134 American cities.

"Albert Kahn was one of the best men I ever knew," replied Ford. "The fruits of his genius are in every part of the world. He was a man of fine taste, the soul of integrity, a public-spirited citizen, and absolutely loyal to principle. He will be missed as a man and as a helper of great enterprises."

During the service Albert's good friend the Rabbi Dr. Leo Franklin recalled an incident that was typical of Albert Kahn. The original Temple Beth El was going to have an addition—a new front entrance featuring pillars. Someone suggested that a new facade should be added to the older sides of the building to make them look as new as the addition. Albert bristled at the thought of creating a false appearance that had no useful function other than to fool the eye, said Dr. Franklin. He quoted Albert as having said, "If you wish to build the house of

God as a sham you may hire another architect, not me." Dr. Franklin added: Albert insisted, "in the house of God there must be no sham, no show. It must be real. It must be what it purports to be."

Dr. Franklin continued: "Every structure which he built had to be real. It had to express the things for which it is supposed to stand."

"Albert Kahn Dies; Famous Architect" was the headline of Kahn's obituary in the *New York Times*. Below that were these words:

"Man Who Built Detroit."

GLOSSARY

Allies: A united group; the Allied Nations during World War II included the United States, Great Britain, France, Russia, and several other nations.

Arcade: An area formed by a series of arches with their supports.

Arch of Constantine: A famous monument in Rome; an arch is a solid, curving span between two areas of support.

Architect: A person who designs buildings and gives advice on construction.

Arts and Crafts: A style of architecture that emphasizes simplicity, respect for natural materials, and use of characteristics of the regional landscape. Architects associated with the Arts and Crafts movement designed not only houses, but also interior detailing, furniture, lighting fixtures, and even doornobs and hinges.

Ballustrde: A railing with a top rail (often a handrail) above a series of miniature columns (called balusters).

Bay: Portion of a building jutting out between adjacent columns.

Bay window: Window in a wall that projects outward from surrounding walls.

Blueprint: A print detailing design plans, with white lines on blue paper.

Chateau (plural, chateaux): Originally the French word for castle, a chateau is a country house on an estate.

Client: A person who engages the services or advice of a professional.

Commission: A contract and payment for professional services.

Cylindrical: Shaped like a tube.

Drafter: A person who works for an architect and draws, or drafts, the design.

Drawing board: An oversized board or desk used for sketching ideas. It is often made to tilt, giving users a better view of their work.

Dry goods: Clothing that is ready to wear.

Emigrate: To move from one country to live in another country.

Engineering: The application of science and mathematics to create or improve products.

Facade: The face of a building.

Functional design: A design that addresses the specific purpose of a structure.

Gaslight: Light made by burning illuminating gas; a common form of home and street lighting before electric light came into wide use in the late 1800s.

Import: To bring items from one country to another to sell.

Industrialization: The use of machinery to produce items.

Manufacture: To make products by hand or machinery.

Masonry: Stone or brick laid by a skilled expert, called a mason.

Mill: A building used for manufacturing; the word mill was replaced by "factory" to describe industrial manufacturing, and mill is commonly used nowadays to describe a building where grains are stored and prepared.

Office manager: A person who oversees the work conducted in a business office.

Patent: The official registration of an invention; the inventor of a patent gains exclusive right to use it and to allow others to use the invention, often for a fee.

Portico: An entrance porch.

Prairie style: A style of architecture associated with Frank Lloyd Wright, a contemporary of Albert Kahn. Wright created the philosophy of "organic architecture," the belief that buildings should be based on their natural surroundings in appearance and in the materials used for construction.

Renaissance architecture: The word *renaissance* means "rebirth," and the Renaissance as a historical term refers to a series of cultural movements in the 14th, 15th, and 16th centuries that began in Italy and eventually expanded throughout western Europe. Renaissance architecture utilized and modernized styles of ancient Greece and Rome.

Resourcefulness: The ability to come up with creative solutions to problems, using whatever tools you already have.

Restoration: To return an old or damaged object to its original state.

Scale model: A smaller version of a larger thing; a toy car can be considered a scale model if it has the same exact dimensions on a smaller scale as a real car. The plans created by an architect are used by construction workers to build a structure. But first the designer builds a scale model to make sure that the plans are perfect so the building will actually stand up.

Specifications: A precise description of materials and workmanship by an architect regarding a design, which builders use during construction.

Terra cotta: Fire-hardened clay that can be glazed for decorative purposes. In the 1890s, architects across the United States began using steel to form skeleton framing of a building, and the skeleton was covered with a skin of stone and glazed terra-cotta.

Tudor style: An English form of architecture characterized by flat arches, shallow moldings, and extensive paneling.

Villa: A large rural home or estate.

Some of the Kahn-Designed Buildings in Southeastern Michigan

Original name of building (date completed) and location

Downtown Detroit

Detroit Free Press (1925), Lafayette at Washington Blvd.
Original exterior remains. This building is on the site of the original headquarters of Albert Kahn's firm.

Detroit News (1915), Fort and Second
Original exterior still evident, including the ground-level arcade style Kahn adapted later for the General Motors and the Fisher buildings. Also notice the sculptures and reliefs along upper facade of the building that relate to the history of journalism.

Detroit Police Headquarters (1921), Beaubien between Macomb and Clinton
Exterior is preserved. The surrounding landscape and interior have been altered significantly.

Detroit Trust Company (1915), Fort between Shelby and Third
Now a Comerica Bank branch in the lobby. The building has been modernized, but the large pillars in front remain intact.

National Bank Building (1922), Woodward at Cadillac Square
Now the National City Building. The exterior is preserved, but much of the interior lobby has been altered.

National Theater (1910), Monroe at Farmer

Once an entertainment palace, now in disrepair. Hints of the original entrance and some ceiling ornamentation inside are still visible.

Detroit Entertainment District and Cultural Center

Albert Kahn House (1907), Mack Avenue at John R.

Now home of the Urban League. The exterior look is basically unaltered, but the landscaping, which Kahn considered part of the overall design, is much different. Many interior features have been preserved.

Detroit Athletic Club (1915), Madison Avenue

Retains much of the original style inside and out, which Kahn based on palaces and villas he sketched in 1912 during a tour of Italy.

Maccabees Building (1927), Woodward at Farnsworth

Now the Detroit Public Schools building. Still retains much of its original exterior appearance.

S. S. Kresge Administration Building (1929), Third Avenue

One of Kahn's favorite styles—a tower with supporting side wings—is evident in this building, which also incorporates elements of Art Deco.

S. S. Kresge Ofice Tower (1914), Adams at Grand Circus Park

The tallest Kahn-designed building at the time; the structure has been altered, but the hints of how Kahn used terra cotta to soften a building's appearance are still evident.

Temple Beth-El (1903), Woodward near Edmund

Now the Bonstelle Theater. The building is radically altered, but the dome and the capital remain.

New Center Area

Fisher Building (1928), West Grand Blvd. at Second
Still considered Detroit's largest work of art. The exterior remains intact, from the ground-floor arcade to the bright angled roof. Much of the interior flavor remains, though the fish pond is gone.

General Motors Building (1922), West Grand Blvd. at Second
New home of State of Michigan offices. The exterior is intact, with its projecting wings, ground-level arcades, and entrance portico. Inside, the lobby and the upper floor retain much of the original style, and the many windows offer natural lighting for hundreds and hundreds of offices.

New Center Building (1932), Cass Avenue at Lothrop
Now called the Albert Kahn Building and home to Albert Kahn and Associates, this is the only additional structure of a cluster originally planned around the Fisher and General Motors buildings. The onset of the Great Depression in 1929 halted development of the New Center, which was designed to complement downtown Detroit as a commercial, shopping, and entertainment district.

North Woodward

Ford Highland Park Plant (1910), Woodward Avenue, Highland Park
The administration building retains hints of its original look, and you can still see some of the sprawling factories that forever influenced modern industrial development.

George G. Booth House (1907), Cranbrook Academy, Bloomfield Hills
Now called Cranbrook House. Several significant additions to the home and changes in the landscape have been made, but the original Arts and Crafts style Kahn used in the design is amply evident.

James Couzens House (1928), Bloomfield Hills
One of several Kahn homes still used as residences.

Temple Beth-El (1927), Woodward at Clairmount, Detroit
Now called the Sacred Light Mission, this former syna-gogue has the heavy pillared look Kahn also used in different ways for Angell Hall and the Detroit Trust Company building. The imposing columns of Temple Beth-El were meant to contrast with a more serene portico, perhaps symbolic of the awesome power and sublime peace associated with religious faith.

Detroit: East

The Aquarium (1905), Belle Isle
The pillared entrance way and heavy brick exterior remain.

Chrysler Corporation Tank Arsenal (1941), Van Dyke, Warren
Purchased by General Dynamics after World War II and used as a manufacturing facility for their defense contracts until recently. Much of the original exterior remains intact.

The Conservatory (1902), Belle Isle
The glass dome Kahn playfully based on the massive church domes of Rome and Florence still gleams in sunlight.

Edsel B. and Eleanor Ford House (1927), Lake Shore Dr., Grosse Pointe Shores
Well-preserved and accessible through informational tours.

Grosse Pointe Shores Village Hall (1917), Lake Shore at Vernier
Well-preserved example of Kahn's use of the Arts and Crafts style, with sheer brick walls running up to a steeply angled roof with wide eaves.

Hiram Walker & Sons (1894), Windsor, Ontatio

Kahn-designed homes and offices for the Walkers are still in use, and plants and a train station that formed part of the Walkerville industrial town are still standing.

Packard Plant (1906), East Grand Blvd. at Bellevue

Aged but still standing, the historic buildings have survived several demolition plans.

Palms Apartment Building (1902), Jefferson at Rivard

The original exterior appearance, including the balustrade along the top, is still prominent.

Parke-Davis Building (1926), Harbortown

Now called Stroh River Place, the original office, manufacturing, and warehouse have been transformed into living, dining, entertainment, and shopping spaces. Kahn designed the original manufacturing facility that is part of the complex.

North and West of Detroit

Chrysler Desoto Plant (1936), Wyoming Avenue at McGraw

Served as the Chrysler Corporation glass plant through the 1970s. It was extensively modernized and transformed, and the long walls of glass distinctive of Kahn factories were covered.

Ford Rouge Plant, Dearborn
Building B (1917)
Main Power House (1921)
Glass Plant (1924)
Open Hearth Mills (1925)
Engineering Laboratory Power House (1925)
Tire Plant (1936)
Press Sop (1939)

Many of the original facilities have been updated and are still in operation. Tours available through the Henry Ford Museum. Images of the plant during the 1930s are depicted in the Diego Rivera Mural at the Detroit Institute of Arts.

Ford Valve Plant (1936), Main Street, Northville
Transformed into modern office spaces inside while retaining the original long walls of windows.

Ford Willow Run Bomber Plant (1942), Ypsilanti
Continued as a major Ford Motor Corporation manufacturing facility into the 1990s. Operating on a much smaller scale in 2001.

General Motors, Diesel Engine Division (1937), West Outer Drive
Still in operation as the manufacturing facility for Detroit Diesel.

Ann Arbor

Ann Arbor News (1936), State Street

University of Michigan:
    Angell Hall (1922)
    Carillon Tower
    Hill Auditorium (1913)
    Medical Building (1925)
    University Hospital (1920)
    UM General Library (1919)
    UM Medical Building (1925)
    UM Natural Sciences Building (1917)
    UM School of Engineering (1903)
    William L. Clements Library (1922)

ACKNOWLEDGMENTS

This book was made possible through the efforts of many talented people. Kristin Palm researched and sketched out material for the final three chapters and advised and edited during the composition process. Alison Jones helped compile the list of Albert Kahn-designed buildings. Grant Hildebrand, whose *Designing for Industry: The Architecture of Albert Kahn* (1974), is important for understanding Kahn's innovations in industrial architecture, shared an updated manuscript with more valuable insights. *The Legacy of Albert Kahn*, by W. Hawkins Ferry, was another valuable source.

Kind assistance with leads and research materials were provided by Sandra Knight and Susan Arneson of Albert Kahn Associates, Inc.; the librarians of the Burton Historical Collection of the Detroit Public Library; Mary J. Wallace of the Walter P. Reuther Library of Labor and Urban Affairs, Wayne State University; Linda Skolarus of the Research Center at the Henry Ford Museum and Greenfield Village; Kathy Marquis and Karen L. Jania of the Bentley Historical Library, University of Michigan; Ann Sinfield of the University of Michigan Museum of Art; Ann Fitzpatrick of the Edsel and Eleanor Ford House; Amy James of the Cranbrook Archives; and Gene Meadows of Meadows & Co. Photography.

Thank you to Daniel Weizmann for insight and advice on the manuscript. And special thanks to Alice Nigoghosian, who initiated this project, provided encouragement and helpful suggestions, and showed great patience during the composition process, and to Kathryn Wildfong for expert guidance through the final phases.

And always, with love, Mary Claire, and Mom and Dad.